A Tale of Two Fields

A Personal Journey Out of Legalism

H. Dale Lloyd

authorHOUSE®

AuthorHouse™
1663 Liberty Drive
Bloomington, IN 47403
www.authorhouse.com
Phone: 1-800-839-8640

© 2009 H. Dale Lloyd. All rights reserved.

No part of this book may be reproduced, stored in a retrieval system, or transmitted by any means without the written permission of the author.

First published by AuthorHouse 10/30/2009

ISBN: 978-1-4389-4940-6 (sc)

Printed in the United States of America
Bloomington, Indiana

This book is printed on acid-free paper.

Dedication

Darline Chancy Lloyd

Haiti's most beautiful child-
Now my dearest daughter.

The delightful & mischievous embodiment-
The incarnate reality of the second field.

"Rock on- Island Girl"

Before you read.

Professional writers, a claim I most certainly cannot and do not make, tell us that the first writing of a thing needs to be free of analysis so as to represent the purest possible expression of gut-level reality, transparency and honesty.

The wisdom is that you write first from the "gut" and then submit it to the head.

I say that the tragedy is by the end of the analysis and by the time the ninth, tenth or eleventh rewrite is finally off to the publisher, the "guts" is pretty much entirely cut out of the document. We are left with conclusions and projections totally clean of any life experience and reflecting only that "head" intellectualism which may be "legally or politically correct"- a hollow, cold shell without soul.

Strongly intended in the book you now hold are distinct and definite 'gutturals'. For this there is no apology- and yet I hope there is humility. The "head-work" I leave to others.

Before you continue to read.

I have considered that there might be some measurable advantage afforded readers if the writer were to include some brief expression of what was not intended in the writing. To so suggest is not to reflect negatively upon the intelligence of the reader.

In my case it is more of a confession of my own certain inability in the effluent use of words, resulting in a particular inhibition in communicating the true intention of my heart. What is not intended in the written expression you hold is any endorsement of that raw and much romanticised "American" individualism which marches across frontiers, crossing oceans, or roaring into space, mowing down and rolling over everything that dares to be different in expression and purpose to that individualism.

It is difficult to discern individuality and individualism when the line between them may be extremely thin and rather invisible; when, in fact, they are worlds apart and to confuse them is deadly. In my use of the word individuality I am referring to that inexhaustible array of differences and distinctions which make each of us wonderfully unique, which mirrors the infinite, creative genius of the Creator. This uniqueness is designed to enhance community and is itself enhanced by and realized within relationship and within the gifting of the individual by the Creator God.

Individualism on the other hand is an organized structure of thought - a philosophy (conscious or unconscious) regarding the definition of self which places self at the centre of all reality and is expressed in and defined by personal, individual rights. The individual in isolation of the whole becomes the whole. In this place all community is lost and each "man" becomes a law unto himself doing what is right in his own eyes with absolutely no sensitivity to anything beyond the definition of perceived personal need which for the most part is self-serving lust. (Daniel 4:30). In this position every possible evil becomes rationally justifiable because the "moral compass" is self-made. And the most heard expression of that justification is, "I am just being me. I am just being an individual."

Understanding that the expressions beyond this point are not intended to embrace individualism as described above please continue to read.

Foreword by
E. Dennis Horton

I am deeply honoured to be asked to perform the task of writing the forward to this book authored by my only covenant friend. I have never encountered an individual who is as much at ease in the spirit as in the natural, and freely moves from one to the other—a rare gift, indeed. His freeing of the spirit and the marriage to the Spirit is truly an evolution toward the freedom such revelation brings.

As Christians, we live too much below our privileges in Christ, and in the Western world, at least, way beyond our means. Everyone speaks out of their own life's experience and it is those events within that life that shapes our psyche. Living with a situation that most would consider to be adverse, at best, my particular words and thoughts are formed and expressed within those life events. Through living that life, the realization soon came that life unexpressed is an utter waste and that the search for significance from within the adversity brings an expression that is larger than the life that was lived. Perhaps the situation shaped the personality and the personality defined the person so that the expression is greater than what society would expect. This statement speaks directly to the propensity of society to make snap value judgments regarding what it sees as the outward appearance as defining the inner worth and utilitarian value of that expression. This book looks to dispel exactly that propensity to judge what is best based on a perception that outward appearance is all that is important to the Christian expression.

From experience, the journey to and through faith is as diverse as the individual, and within that context I can only relate what has come to be my core faith and within a particular style of both convoluted thinking and linear logic has led me to the conclusions I am about to present.

The simple message of the Gospel is a belief upon the birth, life, death, and resurrection of Jesus Christ as the last necessary atoning sacrifice for sin, and a renouncing of the former sinful life is all that is required for salvation of the eternal soul. It is my core belief that everyone is eternal—always was, and always will be. I base the beginning of that conclusion on three particular passages of Scripture: *Genesis 2:7; "And the LORD God formed man of the dust of the ground, and breathed into his nostrils the breath of life; and man became a living soul.."* Therefore, the soul of man is from the breath of God himself. The other is from *Ephesians 1:4 KJV* " *According as he hath chosen us in him before the foundation of the world, that we should be holy and without blame before him in love:*"; and in God's choosing of the prophet Jeremiah he said that "*before I formed you in your mother's womb, I knew you.*" The human mind has great difficulty with the concept of eternity, but faith says that there is more to come after this passage through the physical. I think that the concept of eternity is often taught erroneously as *coming after us.* This gives rise to the idea that it begins with us when in reality, it continues in us. So, if one accepts the fact that all are eternal, then the passage through the physical is the replenishing of the work of the Creator God and the ultimate conquest of evil.

As Christians (those called in the name of Christ), we will arrive in Heaven faithless and hopeless. It has to be thus because hope is fulfilled in fruition and faith is no longer required in sight. When we live in the realized presence of an awesome, holy God, then we have no further need of hope or faith. Given this proposition, the real question becomes, "What is your forwarding address?"

However, the simplicity of the message of the Gospel of Jesus Christ is not enough for man to leave alone. From the giving of the law to Moses through the Church Age, there have been those that have attached other conditions to salvation. It is not enough to simply accept

Jesus' sacrifice as our own, repent of our sinful ways, and be baptized out of obedience. Gnosisticism was one of the first of what was to be known as "false worship" or a dilution of the Gospel message and it is still alive and well in the modern age wherein so called believers claim to possess secret knowledge of the ways and means of God. Man wants to keep adding conditions to the acceptance of the message in an attempt to demonstrate the superiority of their secret revelation.

The journey to faith and faithfulness begins with a few intellectual decisions. For me, one of the first of those was that I decided there had to be a source of ultimate truth somewhere within the human expression or within the universe. Since no acceptable alternative source readily presented itself, I chose to believe that the Bible was that source. My belief is that the Bible is the inspired, infallible word of the one, true, and living God that created the universe with the power of His spoken word. Anything less than that and I am like Galileo (15 February 1564– 8 January 1642) when forced to recant his theory that earth revolved around the sun as heresy, made the statement as directed by the church. He then reputedly arose and said, *"Eppur si muove!"* (It still moves). Galileo conformed to the ritual of the day; yet, recognized and stated that neither conformity nor his recantation affected the fact that the earth still revolved around the sun. What I think, or anyone else for that matter, affects not one iota the truth of the word of God.

Society has always tried to label everything as a methodology of distinguishing one thing from another. Labelling is a far different concept than naming objects as a means of distinction. Labels are attached to denote inferiority or superiority; or more simply expressed, a mechanism for discrimination. We take great pride in announcing whether we are Baptist, Methodist, Catholic, etc. to symbolize that all others are inferior. One does not have to travel far or listen very closely to hear one group's disdain for the other. Labels only serve to divide rather than unite. As people set about establishing their "label" (probably better described as "brand") the necessity for setting standards or rules for their particular label or brand becomes paramount, and that those standards or rules are better than any other label's. Those rules and regulations soon give rise to rituals and the standard of perfection becomes excellence in and conformity to the ritual. Those that can best perform the rituals become the leaders of the label and within a short period of time, the ritual becomes the legal framework under which the label is legitimized. This is legalism in its purest form. Soon, the promulgation of conformity to the ritual becomes the definition of worship. I am convinced that the power of a cult upon its members is the absolute demand that one conform to the ritual – the worship.

This book is an illustration of the effects of the imposition of "legalism" upon the worship experience. One is measured in strict conformity and evenness and the other comparison is what happens when God is left to his own devices. Between these two points lie what I believe is the explanation of the scene in the Book of Matthew: *" Not everyone who says to Me, 'Lord, Lord,' will enter the kingdom of heaven, but he who does the will of My Father who is in heaven will enter. Many will say to Me on that day, 'Lord, Lord, did we not prophesy in Your name, and in Your name cast out demons, and in Your name perform many miracles?' And then I will declare to them, 'I never knew you; Depart from me you who practice lawlessness.'"* (Matt. 7:21-23)

Those whom the Lord never knew were those that have been deceived into worshipping the "label" or are worshipping at the altar of deceitful superiority – motivated by pride and defined as lawlessness. The will of the Father is that those that truly are penitent will worship Him in the freedom of the spirit that has been connected to the truth through the salvation experience; and that salvation experience is worlds apart from the concept of acceptance of the "brand" or ritual. Acceptance of the denominational ritual never totally expresses a relationship with Jesus Christ, nor does it express the communication of the spirit as we nurture one another through faith. One of the central themes running throughout all of the New Testament is to beware of false worship or idol worship. The many references to deception and being deceived are to warn against falling into the trap of legalism which is always an outgrowth in one form or another of Gnosticism; thereby indulging in false worship. C. S. Lewis once wrote that, *"There are no locks on the **outside** of the gates of Hell."* His intent, I think was and is, to convey that it is easy to get in; impossible to get out. If one blindly follows the ritual of the "brand", a door may be found that is easy to enter; however, hard to exit. The purpose is to point people to Christ and through the pointing, guide the individual into a life of thinking for oneself and enjoying the liberating freedom the truth of the Word of God brings: ***Life in the Spirit; Life without labels.***

There is a story of a farmer that had taken a field that had been overgrown and cleaned it to a state of perfection as any farmer tilling the soil would have wanted. Someone, looking at the work, stated that "he and God had a magnificent field." To which the farmer replied, "You shoulda seen it when God had it by himself!" This little story illustrates that human thinking is tuned to a predefined idea of conformity and what is "right" – a predefined dogma regarding the definition of all fields. The matter of the "logical approach" leaves little room in which God can move in us, and in so doing, move us.

The name 'Christian' should be all that is necessary to declare our spiritual belief system. The sovereign will of a holy God is that He gave all He had in the universe for us, His crowning creation. He gave His Son. His only condition to cure the sinful nature brought into the world through the fall is the acceptance by faith alone of the atoning sacrifice His Son gave on the Cross. That, dear reader, is the true liberation of the mind and the freedom of the soul.

H. Dale Lloyd

The church of today bears little, if any, resemblance of the church of St. Paul's time. More attention is paid to the order of service than to true teaching and worship. We have great difficulty teaching or believing in the concept of a suffering Christ, yet live life facing all sorts of hurdles and pain without ever making the connection that as Christ suffered, we, too, will face tribulation and hardship. The concept of the second field in all of its *seasonal* beauty is that regardless of the state of our perception or recognition, God is working to bring His sovereign plan into each individual life expression. Legalism, ritual, nor religion has any position in the gift of an awesome, holy God.

I trust that the digesting of the remainder of the book will prove to be as liberating to your journey to and through faith as the simplicity of the message.

Chapter One

Beginnings

"It was the best of times; it was the worst of times." With these opening lines, Dickens' timeless classic, *A Tale of Two Cities,* was delivered into the world one word at a time. With no such classic rattling around in the haunted closets of my soul, I begin simply: It was neither the best of times nor the worst of times; it was simply *a* time, *a* summertime, *a* summertime tale of two fields in which was hidden a summertime revelation of two views of the church. The church institutional and the church dynamic. The church organizational and the church organic. The church uniform and the church unique. The church sterile and the church relational. The church as a culture of sameness and the church as diverse in individuality. The church legal and the church spiritual. And in some very particular way this was *my* time, *my* summertime, *my* summertime journey between two fields, *my* summertime tale of two fields.

In this age of information overload words and images, signs and symbols from every nook and cranny of the globe wash over our consciousness through the ever-evolving shiny gadgets of our technology, until the mind has been dulled into a stale fog of numb insensitivity. I suppose we know "more about" yet understand "less of" than any of the preceding generations, or perhaps all of those generations combined. We know how to get there, but know not where we have arrived nor yet how to behave upon arrival. Our science and technology even allow us to explain how individual, personal identity and definition makes its way from one generation to the next and the next and the next. I look upon fading pictures of my long dead parents and conclude that as to material definition and image they will never be totally absent so long as I and the rest of their brood are present. And beyond us, their grandchildren and great grandchildren assure the same.

But what of our likes and dislikes, our loves and hates, our interests, our passions?

What of the things that stir life, causing it to spark and flash and flame and to burn hot with total being-consuming obsession? What of the things that beget dread and loathing and numbness and death? How do these realities of soul - inner world pulses - move across the generations with such consistency? Even here there is a physiological dynamic that science delights to articulate, making the boast that with the articulation all wonder is expelled, all mystery has come to an end, which, after all, were only the marks of our blissful ignorance.

But for all of this there remains a certain core notion that *be-ing* is more than physiology. Consciousness is more than chemicals in gray cells and electrical pulses racing up and down a central nervous system. Life holds definition, meaning, value, wonder, and mystery beyond the test tube, beyond the lab door. Something or Someone far greater than the most brilliant scientist possesses the final explanation of my life and consciousness. And without discounting the incredible value of the lab in relation to that reality of being which is physical, material, body, there remains for me a reality, a dynamic, a definition of being, a consciousness of existence that is so non-physical, so non-material, so non-body, so other-worldly.

Spirit - just as real, and more so than things physical, things material.

Spirit - God essence, angel substance, and therefore beyond capture and containment in the lab.

Spirit - present in the physical but always transcending narrow materialism.

Spirit - filling time but losing nothing of essential reality, definition, being, and identity when time has long since surrendered to timelessness.

Spirit - before time and dust, and eternally present after time and dust.

My mother was Mohawk Indian, and this has been my secret explanation for a particular soul passion, spirit consciousness - something that seeped through the generations and bubbled up inside of me. I have inherited a love for things wild; for fields, woods, streams, rivers, storms, animals, birds, butterflies, bees, and a numberless host of "little things" that know and traverse the tiny, crooked highways through the grass. And who shall catch a lightning bolt in his hand? Who shall muzzle the responding thunder? Who shall gather up the wind and subject it to his will? I delight in what has not yet been tamed (or should that be tainted?). Just imagine it - a whole universe of wonder, mystery, delight, and challenge; a whole universe of colour, sound, and movement; a whole universe of labour, effort, and self-preservation; a whole universe of conflict, battle, life, and death; a whole universe of process and purpose; a whole universe of God-revelation right here at the toe of my boot all wrapped up in a sea of grass.

In the fifty-fifth summer of my journey through summers, it was a field - a silly, little field - that turned my melancholy soul upside down, inside out, stretched it in all directions at once, enlarged it with haunting longing, burning passion, swelling desire, as well as piercing pangs of loneliness. A soul full, then empty - then full again and empty again, or perhaps both at the same moment. A field - a crazy, little field in which the past, the future, and the present all ran together in some blurred indistinction and yet never really lost distinctiveness. The sweet and sour of my past - the whole fifty-five years of it. The hope and hopelessness of the future - its dreams, its fires, its passions; the exhausted limitations of my imagination. There, in that present moment, the past and future met. Both the ecstasy and the pain collided, crashed, spun, twisted, and tumbled over each other. They giggled and danced; they mocked and teased each other, and played.

Of the wonders my eyes have beheld, from Africa to the islands of the Caribbean to the crisscrossing of North America, it is still that one crazy little field, that goofy little patchwork of multiple colours, that indiscriminate mix that has become the definition of so much of the inner reality and soul consciousness of my life. The orbit of my life has a centre. It matters not the breadth of the loop nor how sloppy the lines nor the definition of the flight. The centre will always draw me back, patiently pull me in, and in the experience of the centre I am adjusted and realigned to orbit yet again - each orbit enlarged with discovery beyond the last one. Imagine that - a field passed by and through by others who saw nothing, heard nothing, tasted nothing, smelled nothing, touched nothing, and were touched by nothing; a field dead to them because they were dead to the field. And yet right there in the midst of what was so dead to others, God disclosed Himself in living colour and vibrant sound. Every sight, sound, touch, taste, and smell testified of realities beyond the physical senses.

Chapter Two

Another Field

The journey to this grass wrapped revelation was, for the most part, through geography that had so far escaped the determination to scandalize the wild into polite, disciplined, safe, controlled, and structured uniformity. And yet on my way to wild things I passed through another field, and it was actually in making the journey through this first field that my heart was greatly enlarged to experience, to drink deeply of the amazing grace and divine wonder of the second field; although at the time there was no sense of that work. And so this tale of two fields must begin with the first field - a cornfield to be precise, one of those triumphs of man.

I entered it with care, conscious that my non-corn reality could cause damage. At once and with astounding suddenness it swallowed me - all two hundred and forty pounds - and I disappeared into a sea of green. The apparent sincerity and completeness of the welcome and acceptance was impressive, and it struck me that one could be lost here for a very long time. I considered that this would be a great place to hide - a great place to cover up. All factors of difference could go unseen, undetected - especially if I were to paint myself green. And the subtle pressure of that unbroken consistency, that monotony of one shade of green was exactly that; *I should paint myself green. I need to fit.*

I had never witnessed such profound unity. I was impressed. (Later I learn the difference between unity and uniformity. I become depressed.)

I moved along arrow-straight rows of corn that extended upward at least two feet beyond my own six foot length. And in the process, I was dusted off from head to toe by playful leaves that took up a kind of game in tickling my nose, ears, elbows, and exposed knees. But somewhere in the game I discovered that corn leaves are capable of more than play. There is a sharp and cutting edge to these lengths of green. They possess the ability to cut and wound. They can inflict hurt. And what I thought was a game was actually quite deliberate in intention. The intention was the dusting off - the removal of any non-corn-like residue I had brought into this mediocrity of conformity.

And yet, my heart discerned a secret among the corn, a secret no individual stately stalk would have wanted for another individual stately stalk to have known. You see, there was private delight in that fellowship of sameness, of no difference; that definition of all things alike. There was delight that difference had come among them - a different colour, a different size and shape, a different experience, a different life-form, a different purpose. There was some secret pleasure that the monotonous uniformity of green - the boring equality; the standardisation of all things - had been broken by my presence, raising the possibility in this community of uniformity that there just might be more to reality and life than the single, straight-line expressions in that field of all things alike. For despite all the wonder of that uniform patch of green with its fixed lines of definition - that witness to the triumph of man over nature - there was sadness in that field, a tear drop in the soil, a subtle lamentation within its boundaries for what once was, for what could have been and yet was not.

I heard the whispered complaint of the soil that compressed beneath my weight and was left to bear the imprint of the tread of my hiking boots. Its complaint was not that I had walked there, nor that in walking there I had left my mark upon it. But I heard its plaintive appeal. I absorbed in my own heart the rhythm of sorrow in the dirt, the despondent sigh in the winds. There was a longing to release into open manifestation all the secret possibilities, the hidden potential, the unseen wonders that lay within its dust. The seeds of multiplied hopes languished just beneath the surface of where vision stopped.

But such freedom was not allowed there. Growth in that field was narrowly disciplined. Life in that field was narrowly defined. Manifestation in that field was narrowly structured. Expression in that field was narrowly controlled. Wonder and mystery in that field were narrowly contained. In fact narrowness was the towering accomplishment. Life was not merely a matter of narrowness within those boundaries - narrowness *was* life itself. And for the keepers of that narrowness there was a smug satisfaction of a job well done. After all such narrowness is not easy to maintain. The minute any hidden treasure in the soil dared to poke its head up through the dirt in response to the call of light - the irresistible invitation of the sun to be fruitful - it was met with discipline, chemical discipline, chemical death. The keepers of the uniformity passed through the rank and file spreading their mist of poison.

You see, any plant but corn that dared to manifest its presence was met with the uncompromising judgement that it had no right to life, simply and entirely because it could not conform to the majority acceptance regarding identity within that eight-foot elevation of green. It mattered not what the possibility and potential of the "invading" growth may have been. The mystery of its being, the brilliance of its colour, the addition of its grace and beauty, the delightful blessing of its fragrance, and the contribution and pleasant satisfaction of its fruit -

all were lost. All were sacrificed because it was less or perhaps more than eight feet in height, its leaves were less than two feet long and did not bend downward, and - most importantly - it did not have ears with tufts of yellow silk at the tip. And so the keeper of the community declared, "This is a weed!" A weed, of course, is any plant that is unwanted. And wanted verses unwanted came down to a simple, easy and uncomplicated assessment. Did it look like and did it fit the majority definition of life in that field? Was it corn? My amazement was that control could be this complete, this far reaching, this all encompassing; it could be so exclusive that a single life form becomes the whole and entire definition of all life.

But this fine discipline didn't end there. Where were the buzzing of bees and that genius orchestration of sound crickets have engineered? And what about the tiny songs of a vast world of tiny things? Birds? Animals? Insects? Ugly, humourous, fat, skinny, long, short, woolly, naked, cute, and almost cuddly? And what about colour? But the protectors of the narrowness - the pastors of the growth - had determined that this was a corn field and whatever did not fit the definition of corn would not be allowed into this fellowship of the same green, the same height, the same wire-like roots, the same leaves of length, and the same ears topped with yellow silk.

Upon entering this uniformity of green there was a sense of comfort, a feeling of safety in not being seen. But that comfort became progressively compromised with the evolving realisation that while I might not be seen neither could I see. Vision there was limited to the next corn plant. There was no vista, no enlarged comprehension, nothing beyond the present green, no sense of horizons. And soon enough the false sense of safety gave way to claustrophobic narrowness. The walls of green pushed in and my spirit began to smother and choke within the ever-tightening and constricting sameness. *Somewhere there must be a world of colour more than green!* And that long traverse through nothing but green deepened in me the cry, sharpened in me the passion, strengthened in me the resolve to find and enter that multicoloured reality. It is a mystery to me that even there within that unrelenting baptism of green there was a faint but persistent notion, a trifle of consciousness, a shifting whisper of colours more than single green.

I think there was a moment - there must have been a moment - in that journey through legal uniformity and conformity to a single colour, when I lifted my head and by some miracle (at the time called accident at best and demonic manipulation at worst) my sight broke free of present narrowness and transcended the eight foot limitation of reality. In that moment I glimpsed an ink black sky spitting out torrents of rain, hurling out ropes of lightning, and shouting out bellows of thunder. Such a display of uncontrolled power intimidated me into cowering back within present definition. But I also caught the sight of something else, something all mysterious and full of wonder. It happened when a persistent burst of light tore a gaping hole in the canvas of black, and against that backdrop of intimidating blackness and with defiant boldness there suddenly appeared the embodiment of my timid imaginings - a stunning arch of distinct yet blended colours more than green.

There was only secretive conversation among the corn about this colourful mystery. Some called it a rainbow but then quickly denied that there was such a thing as a rainbow or that they had even used the term. And so, with earnest sincerity and in the fear of God, I tried my best to honour that culture of denial. I would dream of colours by night. I would confess a single shade of green by day. But in the end colours more than green had infiltrated my colourless soul, and though the journey through conformity would continue long, hard, frustrating, painful, fearful, and tearful, the point is it would continue. Its continuation was not accounted for by my determination but by the irrefutable, inarguable, undeniable, and irresistible reality of colours for a moment glimpsed. The call of multi-colour would extricate me from the one shade of green. Either that or the profound frustration of having beheld it would deepen my sense of death until I myself was dead.

The pain of seeing something beyond when you cannot get beyond is unlike any other pain. I grew to both love and hate that splash of rainbow-coloured reality I had witnessed. I loved its possibility, all it suggested. I loved how it coloured my dreams. But I hated how, by sheer contrast, it deepened my frustration with this whole world of green. If the green narrowness was ever tolerable it was no longer. There were moments when I cursed what I had seen. I screamed into the face of the Creator of multicoloured reality, "Why have You orchestrated this exposure to rainbow colour only to leave me to languish in a world of sickly green?!!" And yet (although I knew it not at the time) with that first peek into rainbow potential, corn-green had lost its grip.

And so I passed through and beyond that first field. And it seemed beyond belief that "through and beyond" had come. While in the midst of that shrinking environment, although there was some awareness of movement and activity, there was no realisation of direction, no sense of purpose, no satisfaction that I was actually going somewhere, anywhere, except deeper and deeper into endless green, meaningless sameness, and static repetition. There is something about the nature of this tight fellowship of hypnotic green, something about its covering height and its long and grasping leaves that disables the eye to see beyond, even when you are a mere half step from breaking beyond. That one small step becomes the giant leap, and that is why that one more half step is vital, although it often is the longest measure of movement. The intimidating boast of the corn, all the way out to its ultimate fringe, is that it is all of reality and that it goes on forever. And I had been convinced there was no way out of this company of sameness. Same life-form. Same purpose. Same process. Same colour. Same size. Same shape. Same scent. Same structure. Same fruit. And most of all, a whole community dominated by the same big ears with obnoxious yellow hairy tufts!

Chapter Three

Relationship With the Corn

Was I ever a *child* of the corn? Absolutely not! Was I ever among the corn? Absolutely! I was *in* the corn but not *of* the corn. And because I was always a child of the second field (even when I had no consciousness of it) my true destiny always lay beyond that first field. It was all about what I was becoming in the "passing through and beyond process" on my way to the experiential realization of the God-created and irresistible second field realities already living within my heart. The capacity to absorb, to take in and appreciate these realities was developed by the soul-stretching frustration of the pain and suffering of my journey through the pinching, legalistic tightness of arrow straight rows of green correctness which admitted no variation. Before I could open to the infinite breadth of what was in front of me, I had to hate the self-righteous, judgemental narrowness I had become because of where I had been.

Failure to understand this - failure to see and to embrace the God-purpose in the passage through the first field - would have left me with a seething ferment of resentment and hostility, an acidic boiling of bitterness which would have tied my soul to the corn patch, the place I'd been, even though I had physically moved into the new setting. On one level I would have moved on, while on this deeper level of soul I would have been caught in the corn maze. I would have spent my new life cursing the corn rather than overflowing with ever expanding praise, gratitude, thanksgiving and worship to God. For my mouth to have been filled with corn conversation while standing in the midst of "all things new" would have revealed that I had not forgiven the corn and had not released it from my personal judgement, my assumed right to exact compensation and vengeance. I would not have been interpreting the presence of the corn in my life in relation to the Sovereign God Who redemptively engages all the details of my life (including the corn details), and all things (including corn things) are caused to bring about His goodness in my life. And so I refused to explain my life in terms of what the corn did or did not do. I chose to understand my life in terms of what Sovereignty had done even through long days and longer nights among the corn.

This beautiful amalgamation and redemption of my past, present, and future set forth for me my true destiny and identity. God had seeded something of the second field into my heart long before I was ever a card carrying member of the fellowship of the corn. Eye-hurting light flashed out from the words recorded in Psalm 139. I understood in some trifling measure that my relationship with the second field was a finished work, a done deal, long before there ever was a cornfield of green uniformity. For that reason alone the fellowship of the corn, the fellowship of legal uniformity, the impressive and formidable image and intimidating presence of towering green could not finally hold me. All who pass beyond the first field do so because their heart is filled with more than corn - even though their consciousness admits nothing but corn. All who come into the second field do so as a matter of heart. And that heart matter is that the second field lives within their heart long before they ever arrive in that place to which their heart is taking them. Despite the brainwashing testimony of the corn (deliberate or otherwise) and the fact that I had succumbed to their culture of fear and merciless manipulation, it still remained that I never at core belonged to their fellowship. Though it controlled me, it never possessed me; it never defined the final reality of my heart.

The New Testament writer inscribed concerning a raggle-taggle collection of names, those who have become known as the heroes of faith, those who left their own "cornfield" of narrow uniformity and conformity, those who left a "field" to find a "field", *"And had their hearts been in the country they came out from, they would have found opportunity to return."(Heb.11:15)* Had my heart been in the corn patch I left, I would have found opportunity to have returned long ago, and whatever pinpoint of delightful colour may be present in this expression, this collection of words, would have been buried beneath and forever lost within a single shade of green.

And so I turned my back on what I had just passed through, emerged from. I moved on through this summertime journey of my fifty-fifth year. The sun smiled. I smiled. The confusing newness smiled. July wrapped itself around me. Warm, seductive breezes bumped up against me shaking off and carrying away the pollen of corn silk, remnants of yesterday's experience; tagalongs of a journey never to be made again. Summer reached out for me. Summer drew me into the unfolding and enfolding mysteries of her soul. Summer accepted me. Her hands and arms were laden with prophetic indications that were wild and crazy, chilling and thrilling, scary and delicious, all multicoloured and infinitely taller than eight feet.

Is this written to normalize others' experience as captured in …

Chapter Four

Transition

I wish I could report that I stepped directly from the first field into the second field. Such was not the case; such is never the case. After all, the immaturity and arrested development that emerges from years of legalistic smallness leaves us unqualified to be entrusted with the heady responsibility of "all things new". In actual physical distance this was a polite journey of three to five kilometres. In spiritual realities it was a very impolite journey of many years. The scary thrill of the first baby steps beyond the enforced limitation of corn community can never be forgotten. But the wild mix of dread and pressing anticipation, the giddy feelings of naked exposure and raw vulnerability beyond the hiddenness within the green uniformity were a mere drop in a thimble in comparison to what awaited me.

H. Dale Lloyd

How do you handle without hurt and violation what your inflexible fingers have never touched before? How do you process realities beyond your maturity? How do you deal with red and pink and blue and white and yellow and purple and gold and violet when once upon a time the whole world, the only "real" world, was green? How does the mind accommodate the discovery that there is more than one shade of green - a thousand green expressions, a thousand green structures and forms, a thousand green definitions and realities that are all non-corn like? How do you absorb the measure of a green tree when just a moment ago the maximum measure of all green was eight feet tall? Obviously I had no frame of reference for the world that now was my frame of reference. It became incredibly crowded in my head. There was no room left for one more wonder.

At first I fought the evidence. I fought the evidence because I feared the evidence. And I feared the evidence because of what it suggested regarding my dogmatic and uncompromising stance with reference to "old truth"- corn truth. The fear was if the corn definition of all reality could feel so right and now be found so wanting then how was I ever to trust my present experience of truth in these new discoveries? While buried within the uniformity of green it is easy to romanticize about red and pink and blue and white and yellow and purple and gold and violet and a thousand variations of green. But romance is not reality. Reality often lacks romance. The liberty, the laughter, the lightness of red and pink and blue and white and yellow and purple and gold and violet soon enough becomes a weight and a burden beyond our ability to productively and constructively process.

In the beginning I just wanted to run and run and run through this world of "never before". It was time to fly and spin and leap and tumble and role and dance and if need be stand on my head and wave my free feet! This was about the casting off of restraint. It seemed right to throw over all disciplines, anything that suggested measure, order, structure; anything that remotely hinted of corn conformity, cornfield control, cornfield confinement. I would *never* be back there again; and "never being back there again" became much more defining than being here. I was looking upon the new, but rather than interpreting it for what it was I was seeing it only for what it wasn't. It wasn't corn. My confession of this multicoloured world was limited to the woes of a single shade of green. I was caught up in discovering muscles I never knew I had because movement among the corn was so restrictive they had never been called upon, never been exercised, never been discovered. And with the exploding energy of these "new" muscles fuelling my run of freedom I was slow to understand that my free and flying feet were coming down upon and running roughshod over wonderful realities. This reckless commitment to be free of "green religion" became my new religion and was every bit as binding as old conformities. There was damage. There was loss. There was unintentional misuse and abuse upon the introduction to life beyond the tightness of crowded corn. There were moments when the whole motivation in my running was to prove, to demonstrate to the corn that I was more than corn and therefore superior to all I had left. "Just watch me, 'Corn Brethren'; just watch me change colours!" Even now I have no real confidence that this "kid with the new toy syndrome" can be avoided. I prefer to understand it as a phase of growth - to be feared only if it should become a permanent state, a long term condition of attitude.

At this point every corn stalk testified against me. That whole conformity of green told me that this is what happens to, this is what becomes of all who break fellowship with the green. The corn whispered from ear to ear of my confusion, my deception, my pride, my rebellion against ordered community. And (as always) they "whispered" just loud enough for me to hear. Like the daughters of Jerusalem in Solomon's Song of Love, the appeal to "Come back." to "Return! Return!" pushed up against my ear gate and clamoured for entry into my thought life with the intention of moving me to do what Lot's wife did - look back. But of what the corn was pitifully ignorant, what it couldn't understand was that the direction of the look is determined by the set of the heart. And so the corn fellowship even prayed for me, at least up until it became apparent that I couldn't be turned; and then it prayed against me. However, some are turned; and many who came out of the corn with me later returned to green narrowness to remain hidden forever.

Beyond that first field and in the presence of "newness, newness everywhere" there was also a loss of equilibrium.

The inundation of colour, the overload of discovery, the weight of enlargement leaves the soul feeling vulnerable as if it were free-falling through something thinner than air. This season of "rootless uncertainty", of apparent loss of foundations and lack of substance was interpreted by the corn dwellers as my personal failure. What was it the custodians of the corn told me? I remember it as if it was yesterday. Good Biblical words poured through razor thin lips compressed with intense and burning passion for "uncompromised truth." "Here is what you are. And here is the only future you have to anticipate if you follow your deception and leave this wonderful world of green." And then they thundered the words of Jude. *"Woe to them! For they have gone the way of Cain, and for pay they have rushed headlong into the error of Balaam, and perished in the rebellion of Korah. These are the men who are hidden reefs in your love feasts when they feast with you without fear, caring for themselves; clouds without water, carried along by winds; autumn trees without fruit, doubly dead, uprooted; wild waves of the sea, casting up their own shame like foam; wandering stars, for whom the black darkness has been reserved forever."* It was the unanimous and authoritative and uncompromised judgement that I was rebellious and that my own sealed future was that of a wandering star. With those words branded into the texture of my soul by the red hot tongues of the guardians of green uniformity, the internal feeling was that they were right; that Jude had written those words with my very name having been revealed to him by the Spirit. *I* was Cain; *I* was Balaam; *I*

than we ought. Somehow this got reduced to the narrowness that we must not think of ourselves at all. And the final reduction was that we must not think. Period. But the answer to the shadows of self-doubt is not to retreat into some false humility which takes us back to the narrowness of straight rows of green where we *prided* ourselves on our ability to remain little but pure, small but uncompromised, few but really holy, reduced but without mixture, tiny but keeping the standards. In our self-righteous littleness we took pride in the words of Christ, "Fear not *little* flock, for it is the Father's good pleasure to give unto you the kingdom." Somehow we never quite considered that to possess the kingdom - or to *be* possessed *of* the kingdom - just might possibly enlarge, swell, increase, stretch, broaden, and significantly expand the littleness of the flock, or at the very least the littleness of the individual soul.

You see, there can be no growth, no maturity beyond the limitations of present environment. Nothing can grow larger than the structure in which that growth is occurring. For this reason the growing baby in the womb must leave the womb or die within that narrowness. The very structure that safeguards and promotes growth becomes a tomb to the growth it promoted. For this reason the cocoon must be sacrificed in favour of the larger reality - butterfly reality - which was developed and established within that very structure which must now release it. Wings designed for flight can never ride high on intended potential unless they break free of the structure in which they were developed. Littleness of soul is not inherent but is created. It is conditioned by the restrictive definition imposed upon it that refuses to let it go. Count on it, in time even corn green will fade to sickly brown. And the final tragedy of it all is that the eye has been so conditioned by single green that it can't even discern sickly brown. It stares into this once green now withered fellowship of brown and robotically confesses green. Even the once upon a time pain of constricting narrowness has by the sheer customisation of long exposure been dulled into the non-feeling of will-less acceptance. In the process of dying there is this mysterious zone where consciousness of pain ceases and the deception of that state is that I'm expanding in life.

And therein lies the tragic failure and curse of that first field. With its single colour, its single height, its single design, its single structure, its single definition and form - and with its refusal to allow any expression outside of that singleness - there was nothing to stimulate development beyond into an expanding definition of life. The message that swept through the corn was always that there was more, more, more, more and still more. "Come and consecrate your heart to receive more." "Come and prepare yourself for more." But the life experience of the "more" was always and only more of the same.

Suddenly I knew that growth had to be called forth by and into a reality, an expression of growth greater than and beyond my own present position. My journey of transition between the two fields was an experience of scary vulnerability. To trace the steps of that sojourn reveals a certain inebriation - an overload of sights and sounds and colours and forms and definitions and realities never seen or heard before, at least not by me. This was so much more than merely more of the same. My knees seemed unhinged. My muscles seemed fluid. My first steps were definitely staggered. Swept along by discovery, I didn't casually walk through the transition one diplomatic step at a time; I bounced from one revelation of wonder to another. If in the beginning I missed the corn, I was soon enough beyond the negative consciousness of my time in its fellowship.

The July of my summertime did not press down upon me. It more and more filled me with light - light that lifted and exhilarated. That crazy soup of feelings of fear, shame, and guilt, of accusation, failure, and disillusionment more and more evaporated. Such feelings - long associations with the past - disappeared with each new step that took me one more step beyond that history. The lyrics and musical score of a masterpiece from beyond dulled into insignificance the single note monotony of corn composition. And the happy and delightful reality was that the future was greater than the past, that the call of tomorrow exerted an influence greater than the weakening whisper of yesterday, and that the pull of where I was going strong-armed into submission any tug of where I had been.

So real was the new, so baptising its reality, so all-being consuming its passion that at some point between the two fields there was no longer any wrestling with choices. *Should I do this? Should I do that? Oh my! Oh my! What if I miss it? What if I take the wrong way?* In fact the whole inner debate of turn right, turn left, go forward, go backward, stop and start became less and less. The journey was no longer defined by what I was leaving - or that I *was* leaving anything. It was now entirely about one thing. It was only and completely and totally about where I presently was, where I was going beyond the "present was", and for what this "present was" was preparing me. At some appointed place between the two fields - a place that cannot be measured, defined, described, structured, identified, or separated and isolated from the whole - at that very appointed place known only to God, I came to know with a knowing (which dwarfed a terribly bereft understanding that could not keep up) that *God is infinite.* Without even a whispered hint of presuming to understand the breaking light of this soul-scorching revelation, I found whatever measure of grace was required to embrace reality beyond my head. I knew that whatever *God infinite* meant, and however that might look in its experiential outworking, its very first and foundational reality was that He cannot be contained in a box - even that particular box He designs for any particular stage of my growth.

We all grow in boxes. And the one who boasts of being box free - beyond boxes - is in fact the least grown. The challenge is not with the box. It's with the graduation. If forward progression, if personal growth is in fact measurable then this is its measurement - the number of graduations we have experienced in this journey from box to box, with each new box being a bit larger than the one just left. The problem is not the box, the cocoon, the womb in which our present development is occurring. The problem is our *view* of the box. That view begins with (quite legitimately enough) the idea that God is at work within the box. It degenerates to the view that God's most significant work is reserved for a particular box (my box, of course). It continues its downward progression with the view that God works *only* within the box. And then with the view that the box contains the *whole* of God. The final expression of this evolution of degeneration is the view that the box itself *is* God - the equivalent folly of concluding that scaffolding (essential to the building of the house) *is* the house. And so, although He is present even in the conformity of the corn, He is eternally transcendent and beyond the scandalous narrowness of straight rows of green.

I cannot take you to the place. I cannot establish the moment. I cannot direct you to a location and say, "That's where; that's when; that's how it happened." *Happened -* that was the notion that drove my frantic journey and forever desperate seeking. Somewhere out there, always brushing my fingernails and yet always remaining just beyond the exhausted, muscle-hurting stretch of reach, there was a detail, an experience, an event, a goal, an arrival which when finally entered into my heart could rest in *happened.* But there in that moment in the presence of whatever I was in I realised that the boast of my heart would never again be a proud "It has happened". That was the perpetual chatter among the corn. This same heart could now speak only "It is *happening*". I knew, from that summer day on, life would be *happening* not a *happened;* and that this *happening* would go on forever, and beyond forever. For forever stops with the stopping of time, but *happening* is eternal; *happening* is infinite. This journey demonstrated that the only real answer to the shadows of self-doubt is true humility, organic within any real revelation and discovery (of even a thimble measure portion) of how gloriously infinite our God is. And in His all glorious infinity and for reasons known only within infinite Sovereignty, He brought me beyond where I was to where I now stood.

Shadows slithered off to that place to wherever shadows slither off. Like defanged toxic vipers that had lost their fearful ability to inject venom into my veins, there was no purpose in their remaining. They could not contest the burning light of the realisation that my standing on the fringe of wonder was not the result of personal merit, of personal worth; this was not the obligated payment for works rendered. This was not earned compensation for being a good little corn member. The reality here was not earned rewards. This was not about brownie points. It was clear that had so much as a single breath of my journey been dependent upon and determined by these demands and perverted values I would be forever held, forever locked away, forever buried within, forever lost among all I was now beyond. The only testimony in my being here was God and God alone. This was a God-story, not a Dale-story.

And so in the happening, suddenly there it was. Suddenly there I was. The journey of putting one foot ahead of the other - repeating the unromantic plodding of step, step, step, step through the fifty-fifth summer of summers - had now delivered me into the grip, the wonder, the mystery of a silly little field in which God inscribed a summertime revelation of the church organic, the church alive, the church diverse, the church dynamic, the church infinite of and in S/spirit, the church relational, the church beyond corporate green.

Chapter Five

The Second Field

More than a few summer days passed into experience before my first steps were realized in the second field. This wild world of discovery was marked off by cedar-rail fences. The fences represented the touch and taint of man, but this touch and taint was very old - the touch of another generation, several generations past; perhaps the original settlers. In fact the fences had taken on the wild of the field they marked off; it was as if they belonged there. The bleaching sun, the penetrating rain, the inundating winds both winter cold and summer hot, the wrappers of snow and tombs of ice had played their part. The faithful turning of seasons of difference, of distinction, of unique quality, of individual impact and influence and ministry brought shades of definition to the rails. They had become one with the grand scheme of the bigger picture of the whole field without sacrificing their individual identity as split cedar rails.

All along those miles of fence there were locations where the wild grapevines had patiently crawled their way up, as if it were a kind of accommodating ladder. Various shades of brown and distinct yet blended green painted upon large fan-like leaves were accented by hanging clusters of fruit so deep purple in colour they were almost black. This inspiration of growth, this wonder of colour poured over the top rail like a cresting wave, and then, tumbling down the other side, hung still in midair about halfway between the top of the fence and the ground below. In other places the wave had splashed all over the up-reaching grass. But pushed by what was coming behind (its own irresistible life inspiration) there was no possibility of retiring, and it simply reached for the fence again - insistent upon following its own growth one wave at a time down long miles of structuring fence.

Perhaps this was the first discovery that laid hold upon the narrowness of my soul. Perhaps this is where the pushing back of withered and shrunken consciousness began. And perhaps this is why I spent so many days and took so many steps - miles of steps - around the outside of this marked off revelation. I couldn't get past the rails. This was not a matter of a reluctant heart. Nor was it a matter of discriminating or repelling rails. It was entirely a matter of a heart that had no history in processing such enlargement. It was the stumbling awkwardness of a heart too little for all that was knocking at the door.

You see, there was undeniable evidence of transformation resident in those rails. Instruments designed and established to maintain a single purpose were now contributing and flowing into and inseparably linked with significance of purpose beyond the original narrowness of that intended single role. It shot through my consciousness like a lightning bolt from the throne of Infinity and slammed into my puckered soul of conditioned narrowness that I (not unlike these rails) could come here just exactly as I was; I could arrive here with such dwarfed imagination that there was no ability to think beyond single, straight-line purpose. Indeed, I had arrived here bearing all the marks and realities of my journey through straightjacket, clinical control, but to continue living such reduction in the presence of such surrounding fullness was beyond possibility.

But the field did not reject me, did not fight against my being there, did not push me away. Most important of all it did not say, "Go back to the corn patch". The field did not meet me at the fence with a whole litany of criteria designed to determine my acceptability into its fellowship, its reality. It did not say, "You are too green. You are only eight feet tall. Your ears are too big. And for heaven's sake, what are those silly tufts of yellow fuzz at their tips?" This propensity of judgement regarding difference was not present within this fellowship, because it was totally secure in the reality of the ever-enlarging revelation in which it existed and out of which it flourished in life. Its bold confidence was that exposure to its reality equalled irresistible vulnerability to its transforming grace. It did not fear nor flinch when difference jumped the fence and slapped both feet down within its truth. This glorious field was not threatened by incoming narrowness nor yet by proud assumed broadness. And believe me, both showed up; both showed up in me.

What a soul-rattling discovery! Truth would not be intimidated. Truth *could not* be intimidated. And the truth was and is that truth is truth; and by the sheer reality of its nature it cannot finally be compromised. This field just stretched out before me, fully confident of all it was. It did not argue its reality. It did not debate its truth. It did not seek to prove its validity. It did not fight to justify its identity. It did not defend its existence. It lived and breathed invitation. "Come and stand in the midst of me. Come and walk through me. Come and absorb me."

This increasing consciousness of transforming grace, first hinted at in rows of rails, now enabled me to caress with my fingertips those same lengths of scented cedar. Stirring to life somewhere deep within me were prophetic hints of change far beyond cedar rails, and I knew the moment must come when my position in relation to the fences would change. And though it was not consciously planned, suddenly there I was beneath a summer's sun and in the full grip of a summer's July; there I was inside the fences.

Chapter Six

Surface Things

If the journey between the fields was filled with revelation and if even the fences whispered profound discovery and insight, none of it had really prepared a reluctantly enlarging soul for infinite enlargement. But sometimes ready or not it still arrives. In fact sometimes there is no way to be ready. "Ready" only occurs within the reality of the experienced dynamic of the unfolding.

That was the frustration among the corn. The repeated message was to get ready, to prepare. But when you see nothing beyond present definition, getting ready is limited to that definition. How many times can one get ready for what has become present experience? Soon "getting ready" becomes a mindless exercise in redundancy. You cannot get ready for what you do not see. You can only repeat what you have done and pretend you are getting ready for something you have never done.

It is difficult to order discovery. How do you catalogue into polite negotiable reasonableness a whole new world? This world of newness did not inch its way into my consciousness one colour, one structure, one expression, one definition at a time. It was like a massive wave that had patiently been lumbering its way over the face of the deep for a very long time and coming from afar. I knew not its origin. I perceived not its coming. But like thunder announcing itself it broke upon my consciousness without apology and without explanation. The whole wonder of this opening vista could not be digested. However, the grand scope, the breadth of this "new thing" was everywhere present and could not be denied. The eye gate was crammed with incoming discovery. In fact the feeling was that every gate would surely come unhinged and dislodged with the press of all I had never witnessed before - all that the keepers of the corn told me did not exist. It took considerable time of my summertime, but the time came when being overcome by the whole began to distil into discovery of individual distinction.

The reality in which I stood had a floor. And within that floor were implications of what the summer would yet unfold and disclose. The creative genius of the Creator God expressed in infinite variety, uniqueness, individuality, difference, distinction and diversity was entrenched in the very foundation of the place into which I had entered - the very foundation upon which I stood.

A Tale of Two Fields: A Personal Journey Out of Legalism

This was not a fly-by-night experience with nothing to offer but the superficial goose bumps of fast moving, ever-changing novelty. There was a real basis there. And the final support upon which all things in this field rested was great tables and sheets of limestone. In some places it was fully exposed. And that exposure was important to me; for it confirmed that there was stability, that I was into something solid and that I myself might finally become solid as a result. There were also great openings, mighty rifts in the stone, revealing the depth of this foundation. In those accommodating crevasses, life flourished. Whole worlds spun within the safety of their walled protection. Increasingly my soul was able to accept the afforded comfort of knowing that no matter what the depth of earth was at any point in this field of discovery, ultimately there was an even greater depth of solid stone supporting it all.

Every flex of movement, of adjusted position, placed me in the centre of discovery. There was a whole variety of soil types throughout this field. Each soil supported and nurtured a different expression and manifestation of life-forms. There were pockets of rich black earth full and overflowing with potential. There were plots of dark brown, heavy, sticky clay which would have been judged by the "experts" as incapable of producing anything. But the non-protesting response of the clay was to simply send forth into open expression all that was hidden within it. From exposed stone to rich black earth to clay that baked and cracked beneath the summer sun to tiny pouches of blond sand. The keepers of the corn protested, "What can possibly live in sand?" God responded by bringing forth right out of the sand, with nothing but sand to support and feed it, delicate and slender expressions of life which stood ramrod straight. Decorating the full length of each string frame were tiny flowers of pastel pink - all soft and warm and welcoming, bringing hope to the eyes that looked upon them.

There were also depressions in this field. During those seasons of abundance of rain these depressions seem redundant and without purpose. In fact during overflowing prosperity, during times of increase and easy blessing, some people even call the depressions a lack of faith and sin. But the journey into fruitfulness calls for more than endless rain. Those low places are vital, for they catch and preserve during times of abundance what is essential to sustaining growth during rainless days. I learned not to despise the wisdom of the low places. And as with every other part and portion of this second field, these pockets of depression supported a whole variety of life-expression found nowhere else in the field. The tallest and most robust grasses were found in the depressed places. Cattails stood strong - bold and erect towers of green, finally topped off with fat cigar-shaped extensions all brown and fuzzy. Wild irises threw flamboyant purple all over the place. Tiny puffs of duck down waddled in straight-line, single file formation behind mother mallard. Things that hopped, things that flew, things that loped, things that crawled, things that swam - it seemed that all things realised the blessing that had been developed in low places; a blessing upon which their experience was now dependent.

It did not drop out of the sky above. It was not written upon the clouds. But if I initially felt giddy and uncertain and shaky just by reason of too much newness all at once, I was slowly and progressively stabilising within this growing revelation of established foundations. Discovery is far more profound and full when supported by an internal conviction of the unshakable reality of what you are standing upon. I was less and less threatened by what I did not understand. In fact the need to understand became less and less needful. The fear of discovery was replaced with a freeing lightness of soul upon arriving at the assurance that even if every new discovery in this field was to prove to be a deception and a hoax, the supporting depths of limestone would remain real. The field had a floor. The "new" had foundations. The "never before" had actually been before. And now, experiencing the stability of that long history, I was ready to forge ahead into this new world of discovery.

Chapter Seven

The Wonder of the Wind

"*The wind blows where it wishes and you hear the sound of it, but do not know where it comes from and where it is going; so is everyone who is born of the Spirit.*"

During my days among the corn I had heard of the wind. In fact I had heard the wind itself. It blew over the corn field, but limited by the locked uniformity within the field and refusing to conform to that uniformity, its manifestation was painfully and shamefully reduced. Our celebration of the wind was more a matter of recalling what other generations had testified of its reality. We even duplicated the reported responses of those generations to the wind. They danced *with* the wind. We merely danced in memory *of* the wind (and not even our memory of it, but theirs). They sang *with* the wind. We sang *of* the wind. They were carried along *in* the wind. We stood in one place and huffed and puffed and declared the huffing and puffing to *be* the wind. And with that self-generated duplication, we imagined we were likewise carried along with the wind. Even now there is sadness in the memory, and I know (in that mysterious centre of knowing) that the wind was grieved, the wind was quenched as it passed over that first field exactly eight feet above the soil. Its burning passion was to blow *through* that conformity of green. Its heart's cry, its whole intention, its long desire was to mingle with, and to bless in its mingling, every part of each stately stalk of corn from its root to the silk on each ear tip. But alas the established green would not.

But here in this second field there was no such restriction, no such barrier to the movement of the wind. I was caught-up by the wonder of what happens when the only control set upon the wind is that which is established by the One who sends it on its way. There was no demand on the part of anything in this second field to know from where the wind was coming nor yet to where it was going. There was no required explanation of its presence and purpose between the fences. It was enough just knowing that the wind had come, and that in its coming it would accomplish the purpose for which it was commissioned in its being sent. This took some getting used to, but growingly I learned to trust the wind itself rather than my assumed ability to manage it into "accomplished productivity".

A Tale of Two Fields: A Personal Journey Out of Legalism

At first I could only back into the wind. But soon, the turning began and was quite irresistible. The wind just kept doing what the wind does. And inch by inch the turning continued until that moment, (oh, who shall describe it?) that all glorious moment of wide open, full face, frontal engagement with invisible reality.

It could not be seen, could not be measured, could not be captured and contained. I could not look into my hand and say, "Here it is". But there was no place it wasn't - including my hand. I knew the wind was there by virtue of the irrefutable evidence of its impact upon all things in this field - from the most delicate movements of grace within the communities of the most fragile grasses to the bold bending of tree and shrub. Arms that had been held at my side within the tight structure of the corn were now extended straight out, then side to side, then straight up - this way, that way, ways that had not yet been invented. Feet that had been pinched within the straight-row narrowness of uniformity began to stir and come alive with the rhythm of the wind. At first just the tap-tap tapping of the toe. But the dance was in the wind. The wind was tickling my feet. The environment was broad enough to accommodate the manifestation. I danced.

One of the new realisations in this place was that even my responses were not a matter of the self-generated efforts of my determined soul. Obviously my soul was involved, but soul response was far more determined and governed by the wind than by the soul. Not that I understood this immediately. Nonetheless the time came when I understood that this revelation struck at the exact core of mere religion. By religion I mean the best efforts of the soul to replicate the absent winds through the learned, robotic habits - habits taught, drilled, performed and practiced; otherwise known as the "corn code".

Even the wind was a wild mix of distinctions. There was, of course, the prevailing westerly. There was also the north wind, the south wind, the east wind. Each brought its distinct ministry of purpose to everything in the field. There were winds so delicate and gentle that they were hardly discernible - except by those who had a long history of exposure to the movements of the invisible. There were winds of horrific strength - violent in purpose, and yet not at all hostile of nature. Learning that difference brought an acceleration of maturity in relation to the ways of the wind.

From whatever direction the wind entered the field I would quickly make my way to the opposite extremity. In posturing myself there I could catch the full strength of the wind that had gathered increase in its unrestricted movement across the face of this fellowship. From here I could also observe, delight, and rejoice in the infinite manifestations of the blowing that was evidenced in the individual and unique responses of the multitude of life-forms within this community of difference. And the greatest wonder was that no two life-forms within this fellowship had to respond uniformly to the blowing of the same wind. There was no required "standard" response. In this field there was understanding that a required standard response always becomes the standard *of* response, which inevitably becomes the definition of the wind.

And so on that particular summer's day of that particular July's summertime I stood, then knelt, then sat, and finally lay down fully stretched on and in this grass wrapper. Huffing and puffing out of the west and rushing over my horizontal frame, but taking time to push upon me in the passing and cause my summer raiment to flutter and flap - and threatening, though not seriously, the removal of the same summer raiment - was a mighty wind. It bent double and triple and finally lay low those many acres of grass. Tall grass, short grass, in-between grass; tough, wiry, strong grass and soft, delicate, fragile grass; every shade of green grass and every shade of brown and yellow and golden grass - along with all other growing things in this grass fellowship. Like some strong-arm wrestler it pinned it all to moss mats on limestone floors. This same wild westerly was once judged by me and my surrounding corn fellowship to be out of control, undisciplined, without structure and lacking direction. There were jagged pulses of fear tied to feelings of lost control, considerations that this wind had the ability to do some real damage. But now, out of realities much deeper than mere thought, I responded, "How narrow, how little, how fearful, how cornfield that all is! So blow you crazy wind! Blow! You are on a mission beyond my understanding."

The God who launched this blow, exhaled, and sent it on its way, was also the One who set its boundaries, determined its measure, established its path, and structured, disciplined, and directed its dance. All is governed by its appointed duty; and it blows on purpose and with purpose - even the wind that passes over you right now. But when the wind brings about results that I do not like and for which I have no room - results I did not anticipate or desire or prepare for - I curse the wind. I accuse it of being out of control, undisciplined, without structure, without direction. I accuse it of insensitivity and of not caring. I accuse it of being reckless. I accuse it of being unfair and prejudicially discriminatory. But the issue, of course, is not with the wind. The issue is with the narrowness of my definitions of structure, of discipline, of direction, of control, of government. And all of this narrowness is determined by the littleness of my comprehension of purpose - the purpose in the heart of Him who breathed. The purpose carried on the wind, in the wind, by the wind is so much larger than my realisation of purpose that the means by which that purpose comes are viewed as the instrumentality of the devil. And even if the instrument is the devil, what of it? Does not the sovereignty of God absorb and ultimately define and interpret even that reality?

But there on that day in that summertime moment, absorbing into my consciousness the life of the wind - its animation, its straight-line strength, its theatrical dance - I instinctively knew that wonder and mystery and glory were passing over me. In the wake of the blowing, dreams long slumbering were nudged and urged into consciousness. Things that would not manifest in the cornfield for fear of chemical death were awkwardly popping up. There was some living connection between the passionate caress of the wind all over my face and the enflaming of my soul that lay just beneath my countenance. It was as if the wind knew that if it stroked my face long enough it would uncover and call out of hiding the God dreams within my soul.

Even the grass and all growing things, along with things inanimate in that community, knew more about discipline, control, governance, structure, and direction in relation to purpose than I did. They knew something about wild winds that enabled them to bless and not curse, to embrace rather than brace, to rejoice rather than reject, to dance rather than doubt. With my back resting upon a mattress of moss I looked straight up through swirling, twirling, living things exotic in their motion and movement. Peering up through rushing air I was brought into the secrecy of the community of flying specks of white. I had been entrusted with a sacred confidence. Right there at the tip of my nose and extending far beyond and seeming to fill the whole of the sky; right there, swirling and dipping and diving and rising and floating and strangely stilled as if suspended from angel's hair, thousands upon thousands and tens of thousands of little parachute-like formations caused the heavens to be awash with white. All feathery, all fluffy, and more beautiful than snowflakes, they passed over me; and riding each parachute was one tiny seed.

Suddenly I knew that tens of thousands of seeds would never have left home except for that wild, undisciplined, unstructured, out of control, undirected, dangerous, tormenting, and violent wind - wind "with no purpose", according to the judgement of those "safely" hunkered down within the corn patch. The next generation, indeed all of the future was dependant upon this "purposeless blowing". And it seemed to me that every tiny seed knew and understood this. They looked so fragile, so vulnerable, so little in the fist of such great force. I wanted to rise from my bed among the grasses to rescue those "out of control" seeds and "love" them back into the safety of what was before this "damnable" wind just arbitrarily fell out of the sky. And yet "me thinks" I heard laughter and little giddy squeals of delight even from those who had been caught up to heights beyond the majority. There was no complaint, no fear, no sadness; there was no dread of the wind. In fact those seeds who had been lifted highest seemed most filled with ecstatic praise and extravagant worship at the possibility of purpose. They had lofty visions of planting their reality beyond the borders of the field that birthed them.

If the wind was God to these parachute-riding fearless adventurers, then they had relinquished their past, their present, and their future entirely to their God. In their abandonment, their release, their letting go they had been pried from old disciplines, former structures, yesterday's controls. All of these were essential and legitimate in their making and development; but now these same structures were ridiculously too narrow for what was to be. Beyond the womb that birthed them, and now swept along by wild winds they were truly free. But they were free within that broader discipline, that enlarged definition, that expanded reality of purpose which transcended the old settings. They were free to reproduce themselves beyond former positions according to and in keeping with an exact order even when that order was not yet apparent.

I began to see this magical relationship between the wind and all things in this second field. All things that grew here had learned how to accommodate and cooperate with the wind - wind that refused not to blow, refused to be absent, refused to be inactive.

Chapter Eight

Perceptions of Community

Summer days rolled on. And so also did the unfolding of the One who created both the summer and the field. But summer was not in a hurry. And I was glad. Each day seemed to drag its feet as if reluctant to follow the sun to twilight and beyond. No day in this field ever seemed long enough. Regardless of the measure of discovery there was never the hint that with this unfolding or that revelation, with this insight or that discovery it was enough; that the fullness of the field had been exhausted. Whatever crowded into the soul today only enlarged and expanded its capacity for a greater crowding in tomorrow.

There were the seemingly rootless mosses that had the audacity to live, grow, thrive and flourish with nothing under their clinging toes but limestone tables. There was a whole diversity of grasses of all colours, shapes, lengths and natures. And strewn throughout this fellowship of grasses, as if hurled out from the heavens by the very hand of God, was an infinite variety of wildflowers. Here was the wonder of all wonders! They brought with them from the heavens all the colours (and more) of that arch of colour I had seen in my days among the single shade of green. Their giddy delight was to paint this whole field with a thousand shades and hues from soft pastels to the bold and vibrant.

And as I raised my line of vision upwards from out of the moss, grasses, and flamboyant flowers I discovered the world of more vertical things. Rising up from the beauteous carpet of riotous colour were the shrubs of individual, distinct, unique and different expressions. Some were slender and distinguished. Some were hilariously fat and jolly. Some were deliciously fruitful. Then there stood the towering oaks all thick and strong. Although they needed their space they did not begrudge the presence of the maples that tickled the tips of their reaching limbs with the tips of their own. And topping off this world of growing things, for they extended even beyond the height of oak and maple, was this other fellowship, all majestic and regal - the community of stately pines. Their appearance was that they had been there forever, even from the beginning of summers. I couldn't look upon those towers, wrapped in black, shaggy coats with their lengthy arms filled with long green needles, without profound feelings of admiration and respect. Of all that grew in this field of revelation none had faced the number of storms in all seasons that these pines had faced, and experienced the resulting increase - increase of growth and strength.

And yet for me these same dignified wonders of life generated a strange sense of loneliness. I think it had to do with a realisation of history. So much history had passed over that incredible field before I ever looked upon it. History is legacy; and legacy is vital to a full experience of the present moment and an even fuller experience of the future. That legacy was inscribed upon and in those pines - especially within the process of their "becoming". I suspected that if I lingered in their presence, if I would still myself, disengage from mere activity, and sit within their cast shadow, if I would embrace and absorb their life and fellowship, and most of all if I would listen to the whisper of the wind passing through their clustered needles, then I would hear mysteries and reap the blessing of legacy. I chose to be mentored.

For one who had just passed beyond green uniformity and legal conformity, this was already enough to explode the soul. How could so much difference exist side by side in the same setting? How could so much distinction be expressed between the same fences? How could so many smaller communities of individual uniqueness live in such harmony that *together* they all contributed to the much larger reality of the single community of the whole field?

That common reality that tied together all of this difference was life; and not just one particular expression or manifestation of that life. Single life reality was everywhere present in the soil out of which every expression of difference grew and developed. From the moss to the way-up-in-the-air towering pines - all shared the same life-reality. The pine tree never ceased being a pine tree. The moss never ceased being moss. But the core, the exact centre, the first and foundational reality of personal identity regarding both tree and moss was the shared life-reality common to the field in which both grew. Understanding that revelation, the moss did not feel beneath the pines nor did the pines feel above the moss.

Before long my senses faced further enlargement as I encountered another dimension to this great interconnected world. Beyond all that grew within this second field there was also a whole other world of life expression in the form of winged wonders that crisscrossed my summertime field from morning to night. The red-tailed hawk seemed to brush the ceiling of that grand cathedral, effortlessly rising upward until becoming a mere speck almost beyond discernment. From the blue dome to the moss carpets this world was aflutter with these winged expressions of life of all sorts, shapes, sizes and colours. Each brought their own music into this expanded environment.

And then there was another community of difference and wonder - a whole incredible universe of life-mani-

was Korah. *I* was the collected sum of all who had failed God from Adam to this present moment.

Bearing the crippling weight of legal judgement I would, nonetheless, live to understand there *was* in fact serious and grievous failure, but that failure was with the community making the accusation. It was the failure of the legalistic narrowness of the uniformity of green. That "once upon a time" glimpse of an arch of brilliant colours across black clouds was not a lie. Its prophetic promise was true. I came to know that the response to the driving articulations of the voice of doubt, "*Did God really say?*", had to be, must be, could only be, "*Yes indeed, God really did say; and God did not lie.*" I came to know that His words are covenant in nature and that the mystery arch I once glimpsed, while reluctantly daring to glance up through my eight foot high world of green, was His covenant signature written all across the sky in multicoloured "ink". Perhaps, just perhaps I, my life, could be something more than the little it was - something more than the corn's judgement of it? Perhaps my soul possessed colours other than a single shade of green.

It is still emotional to reflect upon that moment of my first vague notion, the trembling willingness to even remotely entertain the idea that such just might be the case. To so think could only reflect pride and self importance and selfishness and sinful indulgence. After all, the hammered message within the corn fellowship was that we were not to think more highly of ourselves

festation down there among the grasses and moss beds; a whole universe of sound, tiny songs and simple orchestrations - each one a masterpiece. That whole lower extremity of the sphere of revelation pulsated with life. It was full of movement. It was full of colour - colour that rivalled that of the wildflowers. My days were filled with drinking in the wonder and the mystery of colour that flashed and as quickly disappeared within the grass weave. I was fascinated with the kaleidoscope of colour boldly displayed by a whole variety of caterpillars on their way to becoming butterflies and the changing of colours within this process. How does a caterpillar of one colour spin a cocoon of another colour and emerge a few weeks later from that world of pitch darkness yet another completely different colour - or even multicoloured? And it was another moment of wonder to find the cocoon of the monarch butterfly hanging from the underside of the leaf of a milkweed plant. No plant was as hated by the keepers of the corn, and if they had their way the entire earth would be a milkweed-free zone. But a world free of milkweeds equals a world bereft of monarch butterflies; and that in turn equals a scandalous loss of gentle grace and soft beauty and dazzling colour.

For the most part all of this grand display of sight and sound is never discerned by the busy performers of mere religion. To enter into this world of wonder you have to pause, bend your neck, and lower your head; you have to bend your knees and bow low - even to the point of burying your full face of personal identity in a grass wrapper; a wrapper full of transcendent revelation.

But proud religion cannot bow and therefore is never broadened by all the wonders just at the fringe of its arrogance.

And finally, beyond all that was seen, all that was visible within this second field there was another amazing and quite invisible reality. This too was a community of difference and diversity. Fragrance. Have you ever experienced the inebriating elixir of fragrance? From years of the single scent of corn (nothing but corn, only corn, always corn, forever and ever corn) to this wild mix of nose tantalising odours was an experience every bit as overwhelming, as soul-baptising as multiple colours was to eyes conditioned by a single shade of green.

Some fragrances were so shy and reluctant. Others were bold and prodigal; lavishly indulgent in flinging themselves into the air while praying for the wind to carry their contribution far beyond where they could see or go. They were intent upon being a blessing beyond their personal position. Although each was individual and unique, the wind did something magical with them - something crazy and wild and God-amazing. The wind laid hold upon them, mixing and blending them into a reality of community and influence beyond individual realization and possibility. And in this each became more than any one of them could be in isolation. For this former corn dweller who now stood stupefied with flared nostrils tipped at just the right angle to catch the perfumed wind, the greatest wonder was that in this larger mixed fellowship of multiple scents, each individual fragrance was still discernible. There was the not-so-shy scent of pine, the equally brash and prodigal scent of lilacs matched only by the flaming purple and dripping white of their attire, the sweet scent of wild roses, the more reluctant scents of white daisies and brown-eyed Susans, and the gentle but saturating scent of violets almost hidden within the grass - all individual and yet blended members within a parade of perfume. Unity and community were possible without that cornfield conformity that destroyed individuality; that destroyed that infinite variety which reflects the infinite creativity of the Creator.

And so it was that from that world of little things at the toe of my boot to the majestic hawk drawing casual circles far above that world - along with all living things in between - there was and is a true perception of their relationship with and in the wind. That perception is entirely different from the perception in the corn. There among the grasses and in the mosses below the grasses and in the winds above the grasses - winds that play with them, tickle them, and when no one is looking embrace them in the dance and even kiss them - there is order and discipline, there is direction and function, there is structure, definition and control. But it is not *my* control. It is not *my* imposed discipline. *I* do not order and direct in this field. And the broadness of life without *my* structures, the unpredictability of reality that transcends *my* sandbox realm becomes a threat and insecurity and vulnerability. He who comes into this field, and is actually enlarged by the experience, must learn that most basic and fearful lesson of trust, of relinquishment, of letting go in favour of increasing fullness. He must learn and live out of the lesson of abandonment of himself to a reality infinitely larger than himself. He must learn this or he will return to the fellowship of the corn, pontificating a terrible renunciation of the second field - a renunciation essential to his being accepted back into corn confinement.

Why is something out of order simply because my order can't order it? Why is function illegitimate simply because it functions outside of the scandalous narrowness of my function? Why is direction judged as confusion simply because it refuses to be directed within the littleness of my present direction? There was perfect order, function, discipline, structure, and direction in that magical field of things all wild and wonderful. Each life-form was instinctively dancing to some ancient rhythm of ten thousand generations past, emanating from and reflecting the very heart of the Sovereign Composer. And thus, the mosquito that pierced my skin in its attempt to pillage my blood and my extreme response that resulted in its sad demise seemed inoffensively appropriate there. The slight corpse of one very dead mosquito fell politely through the soft air and came to rest upon a sympathetic and accommodating blade of grass. End of story? Not quite. There is no end, not even in death. The living is hungry, and evidently for one living and hungry ant a dead mosquito will do just fine. "Thank you very much, Sir. Glad you came by." With each laboured yank and twist and tug, I watched a poor murdered mosquito, who was only responding to his own mosquito order and drive, disappear into that underworld of mystery all covered over with grass. That night the ant family gave thanks for the groceries. The mosquito community mourned. And again, it all seemed perfectly acceptable, perfectly balanced and appropriate - except, of course, for the one murdered mosquito (albeit murdered in self-defence).

Order within that field in relation to the wind - process and procedure within the "becoming" of all things - was declared to be blasphemous disorder within the staid uniformity of the corn. But before summer's end my own soul had come to a rock solid conviction that the rigidly controlled order within the green uniformity of the corn fellowship was the order of diminishment, the order of decrease, the order of shrinkage, the order of pinching narrowness - which, in the end, is the order of death. The dream dies. Potential withers. Possibility hides its face. Hope weeps. Faith languishes. Anticipation flees. Reaching draws back. Vision dims. Daring dulls. "I can" becomes "I can't." And the disillusioned heart - with hope once too often deferred - finally succumbs to green singleness and sighs in dead monotone, "I...really...love...green..." And that is the crippling tragedy of stall, of stalemate and stagnation. The soul that was once upon a time vibrant and dynamic becomes a bitter stench of ferment. The eye that was once wonder-wide and filled with "much more beyond" becomes tragically narrowed into a squeezed and pinched perpetual squint. The ear once sensitive to far-off sounds beyond the corn becomes deaf to all it once discerned. The spirit once aglow with living visions of advancing heroism retreats into an "honourable withdrawal", a forced retirement.

H. Dale Lloyd

As I stood in the centre of that field, for some strange and inexplicable reason I had the feeling that that field stood at the centre of my reality and consciousness. All alone in the centre of that patch of organic uniqueness I was filled with a sure and certain knowing (which can never be explained and can only be experienced) that I was standing in the midst of my life and in a definition of faith that cannot finally be defined and yet defines me - my life, my values, my hopes, my dreams, my aspirations, my passions, my reaching; the core cry that throws off every muzzle and shatters the silence of mindless acceptance. In that God-painted and ever-alive portrait of things all rough and tumble, things all raggle-taggle and wild, things all out of order and yet perfectly orderly, my heart caught some fly-speck measure of the definition and reality of that great Heart that beats out the rhythm that pulsates in and through my postage stamp universe. And it is the same rhythm that flutters in the wing of the butterfly, roars in the restlessness of the sea; that same rhythm is manifest in a hundred thousand sounds and movements in the whole of the universe within, and also outside of, those fences.

Chapter Nine

A Personal Choice

I suspect that the rest of my life shall be spent dealing with the very real challenges of community and fellowship, of "church" in which the single and common life reality of the Spirit is expressed in an infinite variety of difference, distinction, individuality, uniqueness, and diversity. This is the church organic, living, dynamic, relational, spiritual. I made a choice, a summertime choice; but the choosing goes on and on. You see, the seasons go on and on and with the turning of the seasons I hear sounds, I see sights, I smell smells I have not witnessed before. I touch and am touched by all that has not touched me before. And once more I know there *is* more. And once more I know that with the "more" there comes a personal choice.

H. Dale Lloyd

Having walked through my summertime revelation I am a little less naïve about the cost of living in and beyond this second field. My soul is stretched, and pulled, and pushed, and pried and probed. Some days my soul is ripped and torn and riddled by this challenge of difference. There are moments when it seems a foursome of invisible entities have positioned themselves individually at each corner of my soul and, seizing hold of those corners with claw-penetrating determination, they in perfect precision begin pulling in different directions on the count of three. As painful as this can be and is, it is the pain of growth, the pain of enlargement, the pain of increase, the pain of expansion. It is the cost of relationship with the one and only true God who is Sovereign, Almighty, Everlasting, Infinite.

Chapter Ten

Summer's End – Life's Continuation

"Look to see me no more." The words of another Dickens' character set forth in yet another Dickens' classic, *A Christmas Carol*. The evaporating ghost of Jacob Marley spoke these words to his miserly business partner in life, Ebenezer Scrooge. And having accomplished its designed purpose, this summertime of my fifty-fifth year of summers was, in its own ghost-like fashion, transitioning beyond present realisation. I would see it no more. It was satisfied and so was I that it had positioned me - it had postured my heart - to welcome, accept, and embrace the coming seasons of change that would unfold above, around, in, and beyond that field. There would be colourful fall, winter white, and liquid spring. Each would bring its own unique revelation, and my experience within the revelation of each season would push back the walls of my soul against the press of ritualistic religion.

I knew also that in the rotation of things, summer would come again: But not this particular summer. The order here was far more than mere recycling. The thought of this rippled the melancholy of my soul to be sure. But it was no longer a controlling and disabling lament for what was passing away. I sorrowed not as those who have no hope. There *was* hope - the sweet anticipation of all the summers beyond present experience, summers never known before and each bearing its own measure of unique reality. But nothing that awaited me in the summers yet to be realised would eliminate the memory of this summer beyond which I was now graduating. You see, this was far more than a mere memory. This was experience carried forward, a summer's deposit, a freely given contribution upon which all that was coming would build and increase. And "me thinks" that this unfolding shall engage my soul until the end of time and beyond that the timelessness of eternity - *infinite happening.*

Special Thanks

Here I am again paying special recognition to a special "little girl".
This time I will even spell her last name correctly –
Or at least I had better.

Cora-Lee Eisses

Thank you for the late nights, the long days and the patient commitment in editing a horrific clutter of words that appeared lost to the merciless winds of confusion.

Your ability set them in order.
Your magic causes them to sparkle.
Your love persevered in the process.
And most of all, I find the warm fingerprints of a wonderful friend on each page.

The Last Word

Our lives are a composite of the bits and pieces of all the other lives that have brushed up against us in the journey of life. The "brush" of some was so abbreviated - so fleeting - we hardly knew we had been touched at all. In fact, at the time, we really did not know our soul had been touched, much less deeply marked for a lifetime. Many of those people did not even live in our generation. They came to us out of their own place in history - history reaching back to those mysterious words: 'In the beginning God created…..' Through the words they themselves wrote down, or the records others inscribed about them, the ripples of their reality have patiently moved across the surface of the sea of humanity and bumped up against us. That ripple moved through us, and in doing so, left something of itself in us as well as taking something of ourselves with it.

Of those in our own generation - our own place in time and space – who have moved in and out of our lives, some remain. Theirs' has not been a casual brush. They came and relationally 'took up a kind of residence within the soul'. From the place of soul connectedness and within the relational reality that has evolved, their influence is more spumoni-like than that of a mere ripple.

E. Dennis Horton - "my great friend of the south" - has been and continues to be such a friend. We stumbled into each other's lives and immediately knew there was divine purpose directing the stumbling. With clarity and ease, he has always seen the intended "revelation" in my writings because he first sees it in my soul. The affirmation and encouragement he then brings to the often discouraging process of writing and publication is immeasurable. Beyond that, he brings a kind of "down home craft" to my books that weave into them just the right shades of wisdom and insight, born of his own unique journey. All of this helps me find my own voice and infuses it with resolve and conviction.

In the end however, it is not what this great friend adds to my books but what I find of his actual life working in me as I continue to find my way through the foggy details of an evolving journey of faith. Books – all books - will eventually disappear, going the way of all material things. Life, however, will go on and on and in the eternal "going-on-ness" of life, you my kind friend, will always be present.

Thank you for seeing and daring to live beyond cornfield conformity.